RISKY JOBS

STUNT PERFORMER

JENNA TOLLI

PowerKiDS press

Published in 2025 by The Rosen Publishing Group, Inc.
2544 Clinton Street, Buffalo, NY 14224

First Edition

Editor: Jenna Tolli
Book Design: Rachel Rising

Photo Credits: Cover, Artur Didyk /Shutterstock.com; Cover, pp. 1, 3–24 Apostrophe/Shutterstock.com; Cover, pp. 1, 3–24 cobalt88/Shutterstock.com; Cover, pp. 1, 3–24 ReVelStockArt/Shutterstock.com; p. 5 Nomad_Soul/Shutterstock.com; p. 7 Ivica Drusany/Shutterstock.com; p. 8 Nicoleta Ionescu/Shutterstock.com; p. 9 WENN Rights Ltd/Alamy Stock Photo; p. 10 Dudarev Mikhail/Shutterstock.com; p. 11 Mikhail Romanov/Shutterstock.com; p. 12 Avigator Fortuner/Shutterstock.com; p. 13 wjarek/Shuttestock.com; p. 14 Ryhor M Zasinets/Shutterstock.com; p. 15 Alex NITZ/Shutterstock.com; p. 16 Gorodenkoff/Shutterstock.com; p. 17 FlixPix / Alamy Stock Photo; p. 18 Treenoot/Shutterstock.com; p. 19 Walter Cicchetti/Shutterstock.com; p. 21 gnepphoto/Shutterstock.com.

Library of Congress Cataloging-in-Publication Data

Names: Tolli, Jenna, author.
Title: Stunt performer / Jenna Tolli.
Description: Buffalo : PowerKids Press, 2025. | Series: Risky jobs | Includes index.
Identifiers: LCCN 2024007332 (print) | LCCN 2024007333 (ebook) | ISBN 9781499446227 (library binding) | ISBN 9781499446210 (paperback) | ISBN 9781499446234 (ebook)
Subjects: LCSH: Stunt performers–Juvenile literature.
Classification: LCC PN1995.9.S7 T65 2025 (print) | LCC PN1995.9.S7 (ebook) | DDC 791.4302/8-dc23/eng/20240222
LC record available at https://lccn.loc.gov/2024007332
LC ebook record available at https://lccn.loc.gov/2024007333

Manufactured in the United States of America

CPSIA Compliance Information: Batch #CSPK25. For Further Information contact Rosen Publishing at 1-800-237-9932.

CONTENTS

A RISKY AND EXCITING JOB

Stunt performers are trained to do dangerous things. A stunt is a trick that's hard to do and takes a lot of skill. Stunt performers might jump out windows, fall from great heights, or even set themselves on fire in their work! There are a lot of risks in their jobs. They can get burned, break bones, or get hurt in many other ways. Some stunt performers have died while working on a stunt.

Many stunt performers work in movies. Some stunt performers perform in front of crowds as part of live action shows. This job is very dangerous, but it can also be very exciting.

DANGER!

Stunt performers know how to do dangerous tricks safely. They are **professionally** trained. Stunts you see in movies and shows should never be tried at home.

Stunt performers have to rehearse, or practice, a lot. Before they are in a movie or perform in front of a group of people, they need to make sure they can do the stunt safely.

SKILLS AND TRAINING

Lots of stunt performers have been active and **athletic** since they were kids. They enjoy challenging their bodies in different ways. Many of them have trained in **martial arts** and **gymnastics**. They might also have backgrounds in skateboarding, mountain biking, or racing motorcycles. These sports take a lot of skill and control.

There are stunt schools where performers can learn and practice their skills. At stunt schools, teachers who have stunt experience teach students. By practicing their skills, stunt performers get better at what they do. However, even with a lot of practice, **injuries** are still very common for stunt performers.

DANGER!

Actor Jackie Chan is known for doing his own stunts. He has faced many injuries during his career, including a brain injury, broken bones, and hearing loss in one ear.

Motorcycle stunt performers might perform in front of crowds or work on movies with chase scenes.

STUNT DOUBLES IN MOVIES

Stunt doubles are trained to do stunts in place of other actors. When a scene in a movie or television show has stunts that a lead actor can't do, a stunt double steps in. Most movie actors aren't trained to use their bodies the way stunt doubles can.

Stunt doubles will work together with the director, lead actors, and film crew on movies to plan out certain stunt scenes. Even though they may only be on screen for a few seconds at a time, they need to make viewers believe they're the same person as the lead actors.

DANGER!

Some stunt doubles work with the same actors for years. In a series, such as Marvel Studios movies, the same stunt double might play the same character in every movie.

Stunt doubles use wigs and makeup to look like the actors they're playing in movies. They also wear the same clothes.

STAYING SAFE IN THE AIR

Sometimes stunt performers fall or jump from great heights, so they need to feel very comfortable in the air. They're trained to have air sense. This means being aware of where you are in the air during a fall or flip. They also need to know how to fall without getting hurt.

When stunt performers jump or fall from high heights, they usually use safety gear. This can include wires and harnesses or **parachutes** if they're jumping out of a plane. This safety gear gets edited out, or removed, from the final movie.

In this photo, the stunt performers have wires attached under their shirts. This helps them stay safe in case they slip.

DRIVING SKILLS

Some stunt schools mostly teach one type of skill, such as stunt driving. At professional driving schools, students learn to perfect different kinds of driving tricks.

For example, they can learn how to drift, which is when a driver steers the car in a certain way to make it slide. Stunt drivers also learn how to drive backward and how to perform high-speed chases. They also learn how to hit, or touch, certain targets in the car. This skill is needed for movie scenes, such as car chases. Stunt performers need to hit their marks perfectly during filming.

Directors use special **equipment** to help film car chases. This is a photo from the set of the James Bond movie *No Time to Die* in 2021.

WORKING WITH FIRE

Lots of action movies have stunts that include fire. Stunt performers might be near a real fire or explosion for a scene. They may even be on fire themselves. Some stunt performers become **experts** in working with fire.

Stunt performers use special products to protect themselves from fire. They wear clothes that are **fire-resistant**. They can coat their clothes or skin with a gel that prevents burns.

Some stunt performers do fire breathing. These performers spray fuel, such as gasoline, into a flame near their mouths. This makes it look like they are breathing fire. This is very dangerous, and people often get burned.

Stunt performers who work with fire complete special safety training. They also learn how to keep the people around them safe.

PLANNING STUNTS

It is important that all stunts be planned by a professional. People who plan stunts are called stunt coordinators. Stunt coordinators figure out how stunts will be done and help the performers prepare for them.

The most important responsibility for stunt coordinators is keeping performers safe. Before a stunt starts, stunt coordinators check all their equipment to make sure it works correctly. Safety equipment can include air bags to stop a fall or helmets to protect people in car scenes. They also talk about the risks in scenes and what needs to happen for everyone to stay safe.

DANGER!

Lots of stunt coordinators were stunt performers in the past. This experience helps them understand how different kinds of stunts are done and possible dangers performers might face.

Actor Tom Cruise works with stunt coordinators to do his own stunts. He drove a motorcycle off a cliff for the movie *Mission: Impossible–Dead Reckoning Part One*. He used a parachute to land.

PERFORMER SAFETY

Everyone wants to make a film set as safe as possible. Still, accidents can happen, and stunts can go wrong. Fires can get out of control, air bags could have holes in them, or safety cables could break.

Today, there are a lot more protections for stunt performers in movies and television. In 1982, a stunt went wrong and killed three actors working on *Twilight Zone: The Movie*. After that, film studios formed more safety committees, or groups. Their job is to protect actors from unsafe conditions. Actors can call them to report a situation on set that they feel is unsafe.

SAG-AFTRA (Screen Actors Guild–American Federation of Television and Radio Artists) is a **union** that protects the rights of people in entertainment. It supports safe working conditions and equal pay.

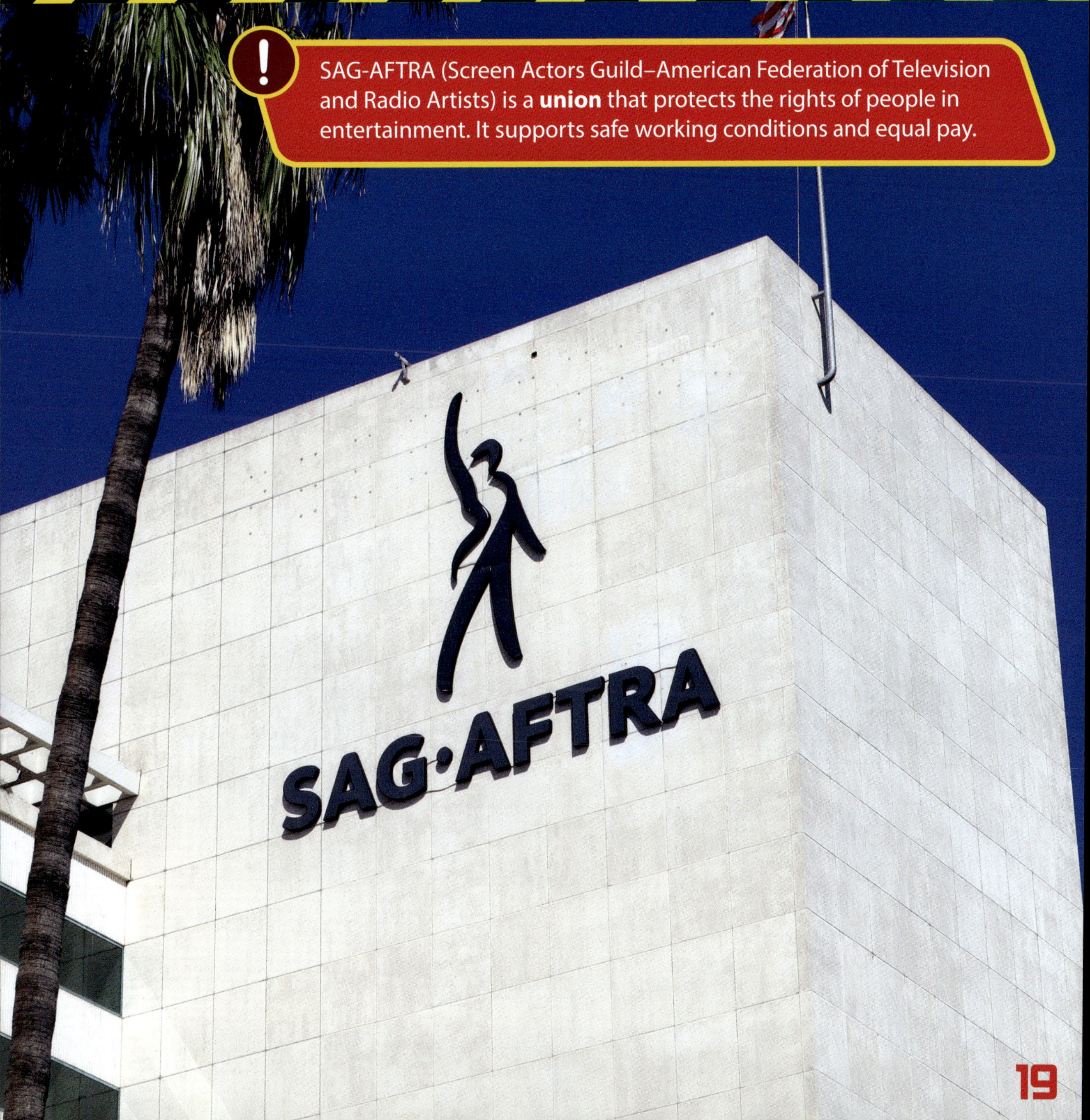

DANGERS AND RISKS

Stunt performers need to be very **focused** and careful. They spend a lot of time practicing their skills. They enjoy learning how to do stunts safely. This could include jumping from airplanes, driving at high speeds, and falling from high heights.

Stunt performers are used to the many dangers and risks of their jobs. They know that they can get hurt or even killed doing the stunts they perform. In fact, most stunt performers have been hurt during a stunt at some point in their lives. A stunt performer's job comes with a lot of risks, but it can also be fun and rewarding.

DANGER!

David Blaine and Criss Angel are both magicians and performers. Their shows include dangerous stunts and tricks for crowds. They have both done **life-threatening** stunts, like being buried alive.

Directors and stunt coordinators choose stunt performers based on their skills and experience.

GLOSSARY

athletic: Taking part in sports or other physical activities well.

equipment: Supplies or tools needed for a certain purpose.

expert: Someone who has a special skill or knowledge.

fire-resistant: Something that is difficult to burn and stops flames from spreading.

focus: To have one's attention directed at something specific.

gymnastics: A sport that tests body control, balance, and strength.

injury: Damage or hurt.

life-threatening: Able to cause death.

martial arts: Arts of combat or self-defense.

parachute: Something shaped like an umbrella and used to slow a person who is falling through the air.

professionally: Having to do with a job someone does for a living.

union: A group of people, especially workers, formed with a common purpose.

FOR MORE INFORMATION

BOOKS

Green, Sara. *Stunts*. Minneapolis, MN: Bellwether Media Inc., 2019.

Rechner, Amy. *Stunt Performer*. Minneapolis, MN: Bellwether Media Inc., 2020.

WEBSITES

Safety on the Set – For Productions Within the United States
safetyontheset.com/united-states/
Read about real safety measures that are in place on film sets.

Stuntmen's Association of Motion Pictures
www.stuntmen.com/stuntmens-association-of-motion-pictures/
Explore different kinds of stunts and learn how stunt performers use their skills and training.

INDEX